Animals of the Night

FOXES
AFTER DARK

Heather M. Moore Niver

Enslow Publishing

101 W. 23rd Street
Suite 240
New York, NY 10011
USA

enslow.com

Words to Know

camouflage—An animal's coloring that helps it blend with its habitat.

habitat—The place in which an animal lives.

magnetic field—An area around an object that has an electric current.

mammals—Animals that have a backbone and hair, usually give birth to live babies, and produce milk to feed their young.

nocturnal—Mostly active at night.

omnivores—Animals that eat both plants and animals.

prey—An animal hunted by another animal for food.

prowl—To move about quietly and secretly.

stalk—To watch and follow prey from a distance.

vixen—A female fox.

Contents

Smart and Sneaky

The sun sets and the shadows grow darker. You are getting ready to wind down for the night. But the fox is **stalking** her next meal. This **vixen** is sneaking through the woods, almost silently. She is searching for food for her family. Back in her den she has four hungry babies waiting for her. She stops. The fox's hearing is very good. She knows when a rodent, such as a rabbit, is digging underground. She crouches down and moves slowly. When she is close enough, she pounces! Mealtime begins.

FUN FACT!

Female foxes are known as vixens. Males may be called a few different names, such as dogs, tods, or even reynards.

Foxes have great sight, vision, and hearing. These senses help a fox hunt.

The Fantastic Fox

Foxes are **mammals**. There are around ten different species, or kinds, of "true" foxes in the *Vulpes* group. Many people think the fox looks like a small- or medium-sized dog. Foxes are related to dogs, wolves, and jackals, which are wild dogs of Africa and Asia.

Foxes have long hair, large pointed ears, and a narrow pointed snout, or nose. They also have a thick furry tail and short legs.

Most foxes are about 24 to 36 inches (60 to 90 centimeters) long from their head to the base of their tail, or rump. Males are usually a bit larger than females.

The fox's long, fluffy tail can be anywhere from 12 to 22 inches (30 to 56 cm) long!

The fox uses different calls and yelps to communicate. Sometimes it has a short, quick bark. Other times it uses a high-pitched howl! When a vixen is ready to mate, she uses a sharp call to talk to nearby males. Foxes can recognize each other's voices.

Foxes also communicate with one another by leaving scent marks. To do this, they urinate on rocks or trees to let other foxes know they have been there. Foxes might also communicate with each other by using their tails. They move their tails to silently signal to other foxes that can see them.

FUN FACT!

The red fox has about twenty-eight different calls that it uses to communicate with other foxes.

Foxes are very vocal. Sometimes they yip or whine, other times, they
even sound like they're laughing!

On the Hunt

Foxes are **omnivores**, so they will eat almost anything. This means they have a wide variety of foods in their diet. They will munch on rodents, rabbits, and birds. They will sometimes eat them even if these animals are already dead. Red foxes eat fruits and vegetables, too. Those that live around humans will sniff out snacks in a garbage can or a pet's food container.

Foxes are successful hunters. They are very fast and can reach speeds of up to 45 miles (72 kilometers) per hour. Foxes have great eyesight. They can see their **prey** at night as they **prowl** in the dark.

A fox stalks its prey. It sneaks up on the animal and then uses its speed to catch it.

Foxes are known for their excellent sense of hearing, but some scientists wondered if foxes had a secret weapon. The red fox can jump high, then dive nose-first into snow that is three feet (almost a meter) deep. It comes out with a tasty snack! This hunting practice is called "mousing." Scientists observed red foxes mousing in action. They realized the foxes were doing more than listening for prey. They think the foxes use the earth's **magnetic field** to help them sense exactly where that next meal is hiding under the snow.

A few feet of snow doesn't keep this red fox from getting its next meal.

Fox Life

Foxes are mainly **nocturnal** animals. They hunt at night and early morning, around sunrise. Usually, foxes hide and sleep during the day in dens or burrows. Sometimes foxes make their homes in hollow stumps or gaps between rocks.

Foxes are great diggers. They make their own burrows or dens. These underground tunnels have rooms for them to live in. Burrows are a cool place to rest, store food, and raise young.

FUN FACT!

Foxes are most active in the very early morning and at night, but sometimes they keep busy during the day. If they are hungry they may do some daytime hunting.

Each fox den has several exits, so the foxes can escape if they are ever in danger.

Foxes usually live alone, but sometimes they live with their families. A group of foxes can be called a pack, a leash, a skulk, or an earth. Usually, they live with parents, brothers and sisters, and babies.

Foxes meet in the winter to mate, or have babies. A vixen usually has about five babies, but there are times she will have anywhere from two to twelve. Young foxes are called cubs or pups. They live in the den with their parents all summer. In the fall, or when they are about seven months old, cubs can strike out on their own.

Red foxes are born with brown or gray fur.

When the Hunter Is Hunted

In general, foxes do not have too many predators. Small fox pups can be prey for large birds like eagles. Coyotes, gray wolves, bears, and mountain lions will hunt the adults as well. Humans also hunt foxes. Fox hunting was a popular sport in England in the 1500s, and it is still active in the United Kingdom and the United States today. Sometimes foxes are hunted for their fur. The silver fox is rare, so they are sometimes raised just for their fur on special farms.

FUN FACT!

Dogs known as foxhounds are used to sniff out foxes on foxhunts. Up to fifteen pairs of hounds work together to follow the scent of a fox.

On a foxhunt, hunters ride horses to chase a fox. While it is still practiced in the United States and the United Kingdom, foxes are not usually killed in a foxhunt today.

Risk of Rabies

Sometimes foxes are thought of as pests or are hunted because they carry a disease called rabies. Rabies makes the victim behave strangely. It can be fatal for animals. Humans can die from rabies, too, if they are not treated properly after being bitten by an infected (rabid) animal. These deaths are more likely in Europe than in the United States.

Foxes can also suffer from a skin disease called mange. Mange may cause a fox to lose its fur from scratching. The fox can become very sick.

FUN FACT!

Wild foxes have pretty short lives. Most of them only live about three years. In a protected place like a zoo they can live more than ten years.

Although only three or four people die from rabies in a year, 700,000 foxes die each year from the disease.

Red Foxes

   Red foxes are the largest "true" foxes. They are about 36 to 42 inches (90 to 105 cm) long, not including their tail. Red foxes are the most common foxes in North America. They live all over the world in many kinds of **habitats**, such as forests, grasslands, mountains, and deserts. They can live around people, too. These foxes might be seen in communities or on farms.

   Red foxes are not always red. In the wild they might have fur that is brown, rusty, yellow-gray, or tan. Red and silver foxes might be born in the same litter. Silver foxes are rarer.

In the snowier parts of North America, red foxes have black-and-white fur that looks silver.

Big Ears and Fancy Feet

The smallest fox is the fennec fox. This tiny fox weighs only about 2.2 to 3.3 pounds (1 to 1.5 kg). Its ears are about 6 inches (15 cm) long! Big ears help keep this fox cool in its home in the Sahara Desert in northern Africa. Their enormous ears aren't just cute. They move heat away from the fennec's body as well as help the fennec hear small prey.

Their bodies are covered with thick hair that keeps them warm when the nights get cold. During hot desert days, the light-colored hair reflects the sun's heat. Furry feet help them walk across hot sand. Their feet also help dig homes in underground dens.

The fennec fox is so wild that scientists aren't sure how many there are living in the wild.

The bat-eared fox looks a lot like the more common red fox, except for its bat-like ears. Its 5-inch (almost 13-cm) ears cool it off, the way a fennec fox's ears do. And of course the ears give them great hearing, too.

Bat-eared foxes make their homes in eastern and southern Africa. Because it's so hot there, they spend the days keeping cool in their dens. At night, it's time to hunt for insects, lizards, fruit, and eggs.

Bat-eared foxes have nine different calls and whistles, which they use to communicate with each other. Seven calls are quieter and meant for talking to their own family.

Bat-eared foxes have large ears in order to listen for insects. Termites are their favorite food.

Alive in the Arctic

The Arctic fox is one of the foxes outside of the "true" fox family. It is also called the white fox or polar fox. They live in the freezing cold, so they are tough animals! During a blizzard Arctic foxes will make a home in the snow. This home protects them from the storm. In the winter, their white or bluish gray fur helps them blend in with the snow. In the summer their fur changes to brown or gray, so they blend in with rocks and plants. This **camouflage** is handy for hunting. It makes them harder to spot.

FUN FACT!

The arctic fox is out hunting at almost any time of the day. When it's time for a rest, they live in burrows.

Arctic foxes eat rodents, birds, and fish, but they like to eat plants, too.

Stay Safe Around Foxes

Foxes are most active at night, but it's common to see them out and about at all times of the day. Red foxes, for example, often live in neighborhoods. Don't be alarmed if you see a fox at high noon, but follow some of these tips for a safe fox encounter.

 Foxes are naturally shy and will probably run away from people. If they don't, make loud noises to scare them off.

 Keep pets and livestock (such as chickens, rabbits, or guinea pigs) inside a secured structure, especially at night, because a fox may hunt them.

 A fox dashing through your yard is probably just taking a short cut. Let it continue on its way.

 Foxes will eat pet food or household garbage, so make sure to keep it secure.

 Foxes may try to make a home under a porch or deck. Try to get them to move by filling the area with leaves and dirt or your sweaty socks and old sneakers.

 If a fox is running in circles, walking oddly, hurting itself, or acting aggressive, it may be sick with rabies or mange. Stay away and call the local animal control agency, police department, or health department for help.

Learn More

Books

Owen, Ruth. *Arctic Fox*. New York: Windmill Books, 2013.

Rissman, Rebecca. *Red Foxes: Nocturnal Predators*. Chicago: Heinemann Library, 2015.

Sebastian, Emily. *Animals Underground: Foxes*. New York: PowerKids Press, 2011.

Zubek, Adeline. *Foxes in the Dark*. New York: Gareth Stevens Publishing, 2012.

Websites

Earth Rangers
earthrangers.com/wildwire/top-10/top-ten-fun-fox-facts/
This site features photos and facts about all kinds of foxes.

National Geographic
animals.nationalgeographic.com/animals/mammals/fennec-fox/?source=A-to-Z
Maps, facts, and photos tell the story of the desert-dwelling fennec fox.

National Geographic
animals.nationalgeographic.com/animals/mammals/red-fox/?source=A-to-Z
Learn more about the red fox with photos, facts, and maps.

Index

Published in 2016 by Enslow Publishing, LLC.
101 W. 23rd Street, Suite 240, New York, NY 10011

Library of Congress Cataloging-in-Publication Data

Niver, Heather Moore, author.
 Foxes after dark / Heather M. Moore Niver.
  pages cm. — (Animals of the night)
 Audience: Ages 8+
 Audience: Grades 4 to 6
 Summary: "Describes the habits and nature of foxes at night"— Provided by publisher.
 Includes bibliographical references and index.
 ISBN 978-0-7660-7214-5 (library binding)
 ISBN 978-0-7660-7212-1 (pbk.)
 ISBN 978-0-7660-7213-8 (6-pack)
 1. Foxes—Behavior—Juvenile literature. 2. Foxes—Juvenile literature.
 I. Title.
 QL737.C22N58 2016
 599.775—dc23
                         2015026946

Printed in the United States of America

To Our Readers: We have done our best to make sure all website addresses in this book were active and appropriate when we went to press. However, the author and the publisher have no control over and assume no liability for the material available on those websites or on any websites they may link to. Any comments or suggestions can be sent by e-mail to customerservice@enslow.com.

Photos Credits: Throughout book, narvikk/E+/Getty Images (starry background), kimberrywood/Digital Vision Vectors/Getty Images (green moon dingbat); cover, p. 1 olga_gl/Shutterstock.com (red fox), samxmed/E+/Getty Images (moon); p. 3 Nature's Gifts Captures/Moment Open/Getty Images; p. 5 Reinhard/Dirscherl/age fotostock/Getty Images; p. 7 Ainars Aunins/Shutterstock.com; p. 9 Frederic Pacorel/Photolibrary/Getty Images; p. 11 Menno Schaefer/Shutterstock.com; p. 13 Robbie George/National Geographic/Getty Images; p. 15 Steve Oehlenschlager/Shutterstock.com; p. 17 BSIP/UIG via Getty Images, p. 19 Stephen Shepherd/Photolibrary/Getty Images; p. 21 Tom Reichner/Shutterstock.com; p. 23 Jeff Grabert/Shutterstock.com; p. 25 Jason Edwards/national Geographic/Getty Images; p. 27 Martin Harvey/Photolibrary/Getty Images; p. 29 Tony Campbell/Shutterstock.com.